Table of Contents

EXECUTIVE SUMMARY

On the night of April 20, 2010, the Deepwater Horizon oil rig, located 45 miles off the coast of Venice, Louisiana, exploded and caught fire, resulting in the deaths of eleven workers. The rig sank on the morning of April 22, and oil leaking from the Macondo wellhead began reaching shore in late May.

At the peak of the Deepwater Horizon response operations, more than 47,000 men and women were involved in responding to and cleaning up the oil spill each day. The workers on the front lines of the response faced potential hazards on the job such as extreme heat, fatigue, electrical, motor vehicle, sharp objects, material handling, confined spaces, potential chemical exposures, loud noises, drowning, struck-by, slips, falls, and insect bites.

The Occupational Safety and Health Administration (OSHA) was part of the coordinated federal response to ensure that workers were protected from these hazards. OSHA's efforts included a comprehensive assessment of hazards and aggressive oversight of BP to ensure that workers had the training and protection they needed. OSHA's activities were guided by its strategic objectives for the response:

- Continually monitor and evaluate BP's efforts to ensure that BP implements the appropriate precautions needed to fully protect all workers from the safety and health hazards associated with their cleanup work.

- Reach out to communities to ensure that workers know their rights and that employers know their responsibilities for protecting workers. Focus efforts to increase workers' "voice in the workplace" and educate workers regarding how to obtain OSHA's assistance.

- Ensure that all workers are adequately trained for their jobs in a manner and language they understand.

OSHA conducted the following activities to protect workers, communicate with its stakeholders, and elevate safety and health in the response effort:

- Integrated staff into the overall oil spill response command structure at the local, regional, and national levels and partnered with other federal agencies to protect workers.

- Before oil reached shore, performed detailed assessments to determine what hazards response and cleanup workers were likely to face.

- Conducted more than 4,200 site visits to assess hazards and ensure that BP was protecting workers adequately.

- Compelled BP to implement consistent incident-wide controls to protect workers from heat stress, the most significant health threat to the response and cleanup workers.

- Ensured that workers were aware of their rights and had clear avenues for voicing complaints.

- Put health and safety information and data in the hands of workers and the public through printed materials and the OSHA website.

- Ensured that training and written materials were provided in multiple languages and at an appropriate literacy level to all response and cleanup workers.

- Conducted extensive air monitoring and other exposure assessments, and evaluated the exposure data of BP and other government agencies.

- Made science-based recommendations about controls, including personal protective equipment, required for specific jobs.

- Established a significant community outreach program to address community concerns and to contact hard-to-reach workers.

Section 1. Introduction

On the night of April 20, 2010, the Deepwater Horizon rig, located 45 miles off the coast of Venice, Louisiana, exploded and caught fire, resulting in the deaths of eleven workers. The rig sank on the morning of April 22, and on April 23 crews discovered oil leaking from the well's riser and drill pipe. Oil began reaching shore in late May.

During the peak of the operations, more than 47,000 men and women were involved in responding to and cleaning up the oil spill each day. This included more than 42,000 response and cleanup workers employed by BP and its contractors, 1,600 members of the National Guard, and more than 2,400 federal employees. The area of operations spanned the coastline from Louisiana to Florida, as well as offshore operations from the shoreline to the site of the release; 6,400 vessels were involved in the operations.

Many workers faced potential exposure to weathered oil, oil byproducts, dispersants, cleaning products, and other chemicals used in the cleanup process. Depending on their assignments, these workers also faced potential hazards from extreme heat, slips, falls, material handling, drowning, confined spaces, struck-by, fatigue, loud noises, sharp objects, and electrical hazards, as well as bites from insects, snakes, and other species native to the Gulf Coast region.

The Occupational Safety and Health Administration (OSHA) was part of the coordinated federal response to ensure that workers were protected from these hazards. The U.S. Coast Guard, the National Institute for Occupational Safety and Health (NIOSH), the National Institute of Environmental Health Sciences (NIEHS), the U.S. Environmental Protection Agency (EPA), other government agencies, and BP worked together to protect workers involved in the response. As a member of the National Response Team (NRT), the Department of Labor (DOL), through OSHA, provided guidance and safety and health expertise to the Coast Guard at the National Incident Command, the Unified Area Command (UAC), and the local incident command posts (ICPs)/unified commands. (See Appendix A for a description of the federal government's National Response System and

Incident Command System/Unified Command.) OSHA's role in the Unified Command (UC) was to monitor the health and safety hazards facing workers involved in the oil spill response. OSHA continually monitored and evaluated BP's efforts to ensure that BP and its contractors were protecting workers from the hazards associated with their response and cleanup work.

OSHA's overall strategic objectives, which guided all its activities during the Deepwater Horizon oil spill response, are listed below.

OSHA's Strategic Objectives for the Response

1. Continually monitor and evaluate BP's efforts to ensure that BP implements the appropriate precautions needed to fully protect all workers from the safety and health hazards associated with their cleanup work.

2. Reach out to communities to ensure that workers know their rights and that employers know their responsibilities for protecting workers. Focus efforts to increase workers' "voice in the workplace" and educate workers regarding how to obtain OSHA's assistance.

3. Ensure that all workers are adequately trained for their jobs in a manner and language they understand.

Section 2. OSHA Activation

As OSHA received reports of the Deepwater Horizon rig explosion, the Agency began monitoring the situation. Under the Occupational Safety and Health Act (OSH Act), OSHA's authority in the Louisiana Gulf Coast region is limited to three nautical miles offshore. While OSHA had jurisdiction over worker safety and health activities near- and onshore, the safety of offshore workers fell under the jurisdiction of the Coast Guard and the Bureau of Ocean Energy Management, Regulation and Enforcement. Despite its limited jurisdiction, OSHA anticipated that oil would approach the shoreline and began monitoring the situation immediately.

On April 22, OSHA's National Office received a notice from the Coast Guard activating the NRT. The following day, OSHA staff attended a White House Situation Room briefing for the members of the NRT. On April 24, the NRT began daily conference calls to provide updates to its member agencies. OSHA participated in these calls throughout the response. Beginning the week of April 26, OSHA quickly deployed and integrated staff into the ICPs and unified commands as they stood up, and had compliance staff at staging areas on the Gulf Coast by April 30, well before oil reached the shore.

Appendix B provides a detailed chronology of OSHA's response.

Section 3. Worker Safety and Health Management During the Deepwater Horizon Oil Spill Response

Under the National Contingency Plan (NCP) (40 CFR 300.135), the Federal On-Scene Coordinator (FOSC) had the ultimate responsibility for directing response efforts and addressing worker health and safety concerns throughout the entire response area. At the FOSC's request, OSHA staff provided technical assistance and support to the FOSC and the unified commands to protect the safety and health of response and cleanup workers.

BP, as an employer, was responsible under the OSH Act for providing a safe and healthful workplace for its employees, including the response workers and contractors it hired. BP was also obligated as a "responsible party" under the NCP to implement a safety and health program consistent with Hazardous Waste Operations and Emergency Response (HAZWOPER) (29 CFR 1910.120) and other OSHA standards. Throughout the response, OSHA provided aggressive oversight and monitoring of BP's activities and programs to ensure that BP was meeting its responsibilities under both authorities to protect response and cleanup workers.

OSHA fully integrated into the multi-agency, unified response to the Deepwater Horizon oil spill at the local, regional, and national levels. OSHA staff rapidly deployed into the local ICPs/Unified Commands in Houma, LA, and Mobile, AL; the UAC in Robert, LA; staging areas throughout the Gulf Coast; and the National Incident Command (NIC) in Washington, DC. Once deployed, OSHA staff worked closely with the Coast Guard; BP; and local, state, and federal health agencies to jointly plan and execute response actions and programs to protect the safety and health of the response and cleanup workers. As part of this effort, OSHA led numerous meetings of the NRT Worker Safety and Health Subcommittee, addressing key worker safety and health issues such as safety and health training requirements, heat stress prevention, fatigue management, and personal protective equipment (PPE) requirements for response and cleanup workers.

On May 3, the OSHA leadership, together with senior staff from NIOSH, NIEHS, and EPA, traveled to Louisiana and met with the FOSC and senior BP representatives to discuss preparations for protecting workers as the oil approached the shore. These meetings signaled the start of close collaborations and partnerships among agencies at the local, regional, and national levels that continued throughout the response and cleanup efforts.

On June 6, OSHA and the FOSC developed and signed a Memorandum of Understanding (MOU) that clarified OSHA's role with the FOSC in the UAC. It also established procedures for consultation and coordination between the FOSC and OSHA with respect to matters affecting the safety and health of response and cleanup workers. In addition to reinforcing OSHA's authorities, duties, and responsibilities under the NCP and the OSH Act, the MOU provides guidelines for information sharing between OSHA and the Coast Guard, including procedures for referrals and OSHA enforcement actions. See Appendix C for a copy of the MOU.

Appendix A provides further details on the roles, authorities, and jurisdiction of OSHA, the FOSC, and the responsible party.

Section 4. OSHA Activities

In the days following the Deepwater Horizon rig explosion, OSHA performed detailed assessments to determine what hazards response and cleanup workers were likely to face. These assessments were based on data from similar past events, the activities workers would be performing, the location of the activities (onshore, offshore, near-shore), and the freshness of the oil. OSHA used this information to help the UC develop a comprehensive safety and health program, and updated the program as the response unfolded. OSHA identified the most significant threats to workers' safety and health and aggressively worked to protect workers from those hazards.

This section describes the activities OSHA subsequently carried out to protect the safety and health of the response workers:

- Site Visits, Interventions, and Technical Support (Section 4.1)

- Exposure Assessment (Section 4.2)

- Personal Protective Equipment (Section 4.3)

- Training (Section 4.4)

- Guidance and Publications (Section 4.5)

- Community/Stakeholder Outreach (Section 4.6)

- Illness and Injury Reporting (Section 4.7)

- OSHA's Support of Department of Labor Objectives (Section 4.8)

4.1   Site Visits, Interventions, and Technical Support

Throughout the response, nearly 150 OSHA professionals were involved in protecting workers in the Gulf Region, with 25 to 40 of them assigned solely to the oil response cleanup. OSHA staff were active in all 17 staging areas in Louisiana, Mississippi, Alabama, and Florida. They visited worksites each day to assess whether BP was following OSHA guidance/standards and to provide appropriate worker safety and health protections. OSHA staff made over 4,200 site visits, covering staging areas, decontamination, distribution, deployment sites, and vessels of opportunity (VOOs).[1]

One of OSHA's goals was to protect all workers in the response. This involved providing technical support to the FOSC to assess and mitigate hazards throughout the entire theater of operation. Under the NRT effort, OSHA provided health and safety

---

[1] VOOs were made up primarily of displaced fishing vessels and crews involved in defense booming, transporting work crews, and other types of support.

assistance for the personnel of the VOOs involved in the cleanup, even though they were working outside OSHA's geographic authority.

During its visits to onshore, near-shore, and offshore worksites, OSHA staff:

- Interviewed workers, documented observations, and collected information on the employers (BP and its subcontractors), workers, and the work being performed.

- Evaluated operations to identify occupational hazards and the necessary controls to address the hazards.

- Monitored worker exposure to toxic chemicals and physical hazards such as heat and noise (see Section 4.2, "Exposure Assessment").

- Assisted the FOSC by investigating allegations of adverse health effects from chemical exposure to oil, weathered oil, oil dispersants, cleaning agents, and other materials.

OSHA realized early on that to be effective, its field staff needed to communicate with workers in their native languages. OSHA assigned staff fluent in Vietnamese and Spanish to the oil spill response.

OSHA applied its worker interviews, observations, and sampling data to ensure that the various controls used were adequate, including worker training, work/rest schedules, and PPE. OSHA also routinely attended briefings that BP and its contractors held at the beginning of every shift to review safety and health issues. OSHA staff immediately brought the health and safety issues they had identified to the attention of BP and ensured that they were corrected. OSHA also raised the concerns through the UC so that they could be addressed systematically across the entire response area.

For example, in late May, OSHA witnessed deficiencies in BP's safety and health program at several work sites and staging areas throughout the Gulf Coast region. These included gaps in BP's heat stress program; a lack of plans for addressing inclement weather, workplace violence, and site control; as well as delays in abating worker hazards and in sharing worker injury and exposure data. Working through the UC, OSHA brought these issues and concerns to the attention of the FOSC and the NIC Commander, provided timely feedback to BP on its incident-wide site safety and health plan, and made sure that BP incorporated supplemental plans addressing specific worker hazards, including the designation of an incident-wide safety officer. OSHA also worked with BP to develop a Safety and Health Action Item Report to track observed safety and health hazards until they were abated.

OSHA recognized that the intense heat in the Gulf region was likely the most acute threat to the health of the response and cleanup workers. OSHA assisted the UC in developing and ensuring the consistent implementation of a comprehensive program to protect workers from heat and ensured its consistent implementation (see below, "Protecting Workers From Heat During the Gulf Oil Response").

> **Protecting Workers From Heat**
> **During the Gulf Oil Spill Response**
>
> Among the most serious health hazards faced by response and cleanup workers were heat stress and heat stroke. Many people, some wearing chemical-resistant Tyvek® coveralls, boots, and gloves, worked 12 hours a day, 7 days a week in the hot and humid weather along the Gulf. From the outset, OSHA insisted that BP implement a robust program to protect workers from heat stress and heat stroke, including work/rest requirements, shaded rest areas, hydration liquids, and onsite heat monitors.
>
> During site visits, OSHA staff observed inconsistent implementation of BP's heat stress program. Each staging area was implementing its own program, and some were more protective than others. OSHA made it clear that BP had to fix these deficiencies. OSHA's Assistant Secretary of Labor brought this and other issues to the attention of Admiral Thad Allen, the National Incident Commander, to ensure that the inconsistencies would be remedied. BP then implemented a system-wide, comprehensive heat protection program.
>
> During the response, there were more than 1,000 potential heat-related incidents in which workers showed signs of heat effects. The heat protection program likely prevented some serious heat illnesses and possible deaths among workers.

4.2 Chemical Exposure Assessment

OSHA was concerned about the potential health effects to workers from inhalation and skin exposure to chemicals including crude oil, weathered oil, dispersants, and solvents used to clean boats. Early in the response, OSHA personnel provided input to help BP develop a sampling strategy to address these hazards. OSHA also developed its own sampling protocol and strategy, which is available on OSHA's website at http://www.osha.gov/oilspills/oil_samplingstrategy.html. The sampling strategy OSHA developed to support the UC was based on the specific tasks workers would be performing, the chemicals of concern from the oil and dispersants, and available Occupational Exposure Limits (see below, "Occupational Exposure Limits"). The strategy incorporated onshore zones, near-shore, and offshore operations.

On May 6, OSHA deployed its specialized industrial hygienist team to Louisiana to provide technical support for the worker exposure monitoring. During site visits, OSHA conducted the following sampling by using direct reading instruments and traditional industrial hygiene air sampling devices to evaluate worker exposure:

- Short-term and full-shift sampling of the air in the actual breathing zone of workers.

- Air sampling in areas where workers went frequently.

- Sampling directly over tar balls, inside bags containing contaminated materials, and in other locations. (These samples did not represent worker exposure but provided information on the types of chemicals that might be coming off contaminated materials.)

The sampling consisted of full spectral analyses of the composite mixture of crude oil, oil by-products, dispersants, and other chemicals to determine what hazards the mixture might present to workers as they responded to and cleaned up the oil spill.

A specialized committee convened each morning, consisting of the lead industrial hygienists from OSHA, the Coast Guard, BP and its contractors, NIOSH, the U.S. Department of the Interior, and EPA. They discussed anomalies from the previous day's samples, updates to safe work practices or administrative controls, and coordinated their sampling activities for the day. This process was highly effective for identifying safety and health issues and bringing the issues to the attention of the unified commands.

Over the course of the response, BP conducted more than 119,000 exposure assessments. OSHA reviewed these assessments and validated them by performing more than 7,000 independent worker exposure measurements, both onshore and on marine vessels. Chemists at OSHA's Salt Lake Technical Center (SLTC), an accredited American Industrial Hygiene Association (AIHA) laboratory, analyzed all of OSHA's samples as well as samples from the Coast Guard. OSHA also reviewed sampling data from EPA and the National Oceanic and Atmospheric Administration (NOAA). OSHA posted the sampling data on its website at https://www.osha.gov/oilspills/index_sampling.html.

The data showed that chemical exposure levels varied greatly, depending on the location of the work and the task being performed. The source of the release was approximately 45 miles offshore. As the result of sun, water and wave action, and other environmental factors most of the toxic volatile components of the oil had dissipated during the weeks it took to reach the work areas of most cleanup workers. Based on the scientific evidence from the sampling data, OSHA determined that respiratory precautions were important near the source to prevent inhalation exposures from volatile chemicals, but were not necessary for most shoreline cleanup operations. OSHA was also aware that respirators should be considered the protection of last resort, as they can be physically taxing on the body, particularly for workers who have not used them before and in conditions of extreme heat. Where feasible, engineering, work practice and administrative controls should be implemented to protect workers.

OSHA ensured that respirators were used wherever the data indicated that they were necessary to protect workers. For example, OSHA noted exposure data from some decontamination operations that exceeded the most protective Occupational Exposure Limits. Upon investigation, OSHA confirmed that protective measures, which were based on guidance from the UC, were already in place to protect the workers and prevent them from inhaling or having skin contact with hazardous chemicals.

Occupational Exposure Limits

An Occupational Exposure Limit (OEL) is a level at which exposure to a substance for a certain frequency and duration over a working lifetime can be deemed to be safe. OELs are always based on epidemiological studies and scientific evidence. Though a number of agencies have established OELs, based on a variety of criteria, not all OELs are legally enforceable. Permissible Exposure Limits (PELs) are OSHA-specific OELs and signify the legal limit that cannot be exceeded. PELs are based on 40 hours of exposure per week over a 40-year working lifetime.

OSHA has previously acknowledged that its PELs are out of date and in some cases are not as protective as OELs promulgated by other agencies. To provide the oil spill workers with the greatest protection from exposure to hazardous chemicals, OSHA worked with the UC to use the most protective OELs from NIOSH, AIHA, and the American Conference of Governmental Industrial Hygienists (ACGIH), in addition to OSHA's PELs.

In characterizing worker exposure during the Deepwater Horizon oil spill response, OSHA compared the results of air monitoring to the lowest known OEL for purposes of risk assessment and protective equipment recommendations. Because oil cleanup workers would only be exposed for a few days, weeks, or months, instead of a working lifetime, using OELs was a very conservative approach for protecting response workers.

4.3   Personal Protective Equipment

PPE, such as boots, gloves, coveralls, hearing protection, respiratory protection, etc., was essential for protecting workers involved in cleanup operations. OSHA recommended PPE to prevent inhalation or skin contact with toxic chemicals, hearing damage from noise, sun exposure, cuts, insect bites, and other hazards.

OSHA stressed throughout the response that decisions about PPE should be based on a scientific characterization of the hazards, including air sampling (described in Section 4.2). OSHA assisted the UC with performing these characterizations for each job task to determine the appropriate level of protection. Based on these hazard assessments and guidance from OSHA and NIOSH, in early May, BP developed a matrix outlining the PPE that workers should use for each category of cleanup work. OSHA posted the matrix on its website at http://www.osha.gov/oilspills/gulf-operations-ppe-matrix.pdf.

Respirators, and training in how and when to use them, were required for workers on vessels near the source of the crude oil discharge. NIOSH and OSHA issued a guidance document recommending that workers in the close vicinity of crude oil burns have access to respirators and receive appropriate training and medical evaluation in case wind shifts or other unexpected conditions brought workers into the smoke plume. Ships working offshore had real-time monitoring capability and procedures for protecting workers when specific air contamination levels were reached. There were no instances reported where workers were exposed in the plume.

NIOSH and OSHA also recommended respirators and appropriate training and medical evaluation for workers engaged in high-pressure washing of contaminated boats or boom and other materials on land. This was based on concern that high-pressure washing could aerosolize the oil (create airborne particles that could be breathed in), increasing the risk to workers. OSHA confirmed that BP implemented these recommendations.

For shoreline cleanup and vessels not involved in the above activities, a basic ensemble of PPE was required to protect against skin exposure, but respiratory protection was not recommended. OSHA stressed from the outset that certain respirators, especially elastomeric air purifying respirators with disposable filter cartridges, could put a strain on the heart and lungs of some workers and therefore were not generally recommended for voluntary use. Furthermore, respirator use could exacerbate the symptoms of heat stress. For these workers, the health risks from using respirators in the extreme heat exceeded the low risk of chemical inhalation.

4.4   Training

OSHA considered training an immediate priority because of the large number of response and cleanup workers engaged in the response, and the wide variety of tasks these workers were conducting. Early in the response, OSHA reached out to NIEHS to collaborate on training publications, materials, and oversight of training programs. Within days of the rig explosion, and well before oil reached the shore, OSHA established requirements for training for all response workers. OSHA also made it clear to BP that all response and cleanup workers would need to receive training, free of charge, and that the training had to be provided in a manner and language that workers understood. This training included the specific requirements for PPE for the different job tasks.

As the training requirements were identified, a series of courses were created by BP, including a one-hour orientation, a four-hour shoreline course, and a four-hour marine cleanup course. OSHA, along with the Coast Guard, NIOSH, and NIEHS, reviewed BP's proposed training program. BP launched a multi-tiered training program on May 5 for workers involved in the oil spill response and cleanup.

As early as May 7, BP had issued a matrix identifying the basic training requirements for each job. This matrix was posted on OSHA's website at http://www.osha.gov/oilspills/ training.html. Crew supervisors were required to have 40 hours of HAZWOPER training and supervised field experience. A minimum of four hours of training was appropriate where sites were fully characterized, minimal chemical exposures were likely, and respirators were not required.

By May 21, about the time that tar balls first came ashore, approximately 10,000 workers along the shoreline and in boats had been trained. Ultimately, in the course of the response, more than 130,000 workers along the Gulf Coast received training on how to work safely.

On June 2, OSHA instructed BP to increase the level of training provided to workers involved in oil skimming operations and operations that required contact with oil-soaked booms, due to the increased potential exposure to weathered oil. This became an 8-hour course. OSHA and NIEHS provided oversight and direction to BP on the curriculum. BP hired three contractors who provided all of the 4- and 8-hour training. Limiting the number of contractors providing the training ensured that the agreed upon curricula would be used and the consistency of the training.

Worker training was provided in English, Spanish, and Vietnamese. OSHA continually monitored training sessions to ensure that they were delivered at a level and in a language appropriate for the workers being trained.

BP complied with OSHA's request to institute a credentialing program, whereby workers received certificates after completing training. All workers engaged in response and cleanup activities had to have a training certification card showing that they had completed the BP-sponsored training program. During OSHA's site visits, OSHA personnel interviewed workers about the training they had received and ensured that workers had training cards. This ensured that site control was maintained and that only individuals with the proper training were present at worksites.

Supervisors and workers who faced increased risks of exposure were required to have 40-hour HAZWOPER training. Instead of providing this 40-hour training in its Deepwater Horizon training program, BP and its contractors hired workers who had already received 40-hour training to fulfill these roles and responsibilities. BP and its contractors were obligated to ensure that the workers' previous 40-hour training sufficed for the tasks that the workers conducted. Otherwise, the employers would have to provide additional training.

OSHA received reports of trainers who were not part of the BP-sponsored training program conducting the "40-hour" training in less than one day and to very large groups of workers. OSHA also received reports of trainers withholding training certificates from workers. OSHA referred such reports to DOL's Inspector General and other authorities as possible consumer fraud.

Training Requirements

Response actions conducted under the NCP must comply with the provisions of the HAZWOPER (29 CFR 1910.120) standard. The minimum amount of training required under HAZWOPER depends on the worker's role and responsibilities during the response and cleanup. Before they begin working, all workers must be trained on the tasks they will conduct, the hazards associated with the tasks, and the precautions needed to safely complete the tasks (e.g., use of engineering and work practice controls and PPE), and provide for actual hands-on training about PPE. After the training is completed, the employer must provide adequate supervision to ensure that safety protocols are followed.

OSHA devoted considerable resources during the Deepwater Horizon response to determine exactly which response and cleanup workers needed training under HAZWOPER and which workers could receive shorter trainings, depending on the risks

---

associated with specific cleanup activities.

OSHA's Compliance Instruction, CPL 02-02-051, provides policy guidance on training requirements under HAZWOPER for workers involved in post-emergency response operations. For job duties and responsibilities with a low magnitude of risk, fewer than 24 hours of training may be appropriate for these post-emergency cleanup workers. For oil spill cleanup operations, where the site has been fully characterized, respirators are not required and minimal exposure is likely, a minimum of four hours of training would be appropriate. Moreover, oil spills are unique in that many people who assist in the cleanup operations may not engage in this activity on a recurring basis. Supervisors and workers involved in high-hazard operations need 40 hours of training and appropriate supervised field experience.

4.5   Guidance and Publications

To disseminate information to workers, OSHA developed safety and health guidance materials in both print and electronic formats. Many of these materials were developed and distributed to the field within a matter of days. The printed materials included:

- A pocket-sized booklet, developed in partnership with NIEHS, containing information on heat injury prevention, health risks of weathered oil, PPE requirements, and general health and safety topics (such as fatigue). OSHA distributed 15,000 copies in English, Spanish, and Vietnamese.

- OSHA *Deepwater Horizon/Mississippi Canyon 252 Oil Spill* fact sheet, which explains basic health and safety information about common operations, hazards, training and protections for cleanup workers.

- Job-specific worker safety and health information sheets.

- *Severe Weather and the Deepwater Horizon Oil Spill: Health and Safety for Onshore Emergency Responders* fact sheet (in response to the threat of hurricanes hitting the region).

In conjunction with NIOSH, OSHA developed the *Interim Guidance for Protecting Deepwater Horizon Response Workers and Volunteers,* published in June 2010. This publication addressed health effects, exposure assessment, medical evaluation and medical care, heat stress and fatigue prevention, traumatic incident stress prevention, and use of respiratory protection and other PPE.

Following reports about seven fishermen hospitalized in late May, OSHA and NIOSH instructed BP on the procedures for requesting a Health Hazard Evaluation (HHE) to have NIOSH fully investigate the cause of significant worker safety and health incidents. This led to nine NIOSH HHE reports covering a wide range of response and cleanup operations.

OSHA's webpage, *Keeping Workers Safe During Oil Spill Response and Cleanup Operations*, available at: http://www.osha.gov/oilspills/index.html, also served as a key resource to make safety and health information readily accessible and transparent to workers and the public. OSHA posted information about hazards, training, PPE requirements, and sampling data. The website also provided links to data, including injury and illness reports, from other government agencies and BP's oil spill response website. The OSHA webpage put health and safety information, in multiple languages, into the hands of workers.

OSHA initially used its own contractors to assist with translating guidance documents into the workers' primary languages, but later employed resources from the Department of State.

4.6   Community/Stakeholder Outreach

OSHA worked closely with other federal agencies to establish an extensive outreach program to engage a wide range of audiences that included local communities, nongovernmental organizations, state health departments, and union representatives. Through this outreach program, OSHA helped address the safety and health concerns of community organizations.

Although OSHA activities typically focus on worksites, OSHA recognized the need for community involvement and dedicated staff to conduct outreach efforts throughout the region. These individuals reached out to community organizations and other stakeholders, hearing concerns, answering questions, and communicating findings. The outreach took a variety of forms, including numerous town hall meetings and face-to-face meetings. In addition, daily conference calls provided worker safety updates to the governors of the Gulf coast states, mayors and local elected officials, and members of Congress. Weekly calls established communication and dialogue with state health departments, environmental organizations, worker organizations, and academic experts.

OSHA also distributed more than 35,000 pamphlets and other educational materials to communities regarding the hazards facing response and cleanup workers. In addition, OSHA encouraged the public to use OSHA's hotline (1-800-321-OSHA) and e-correspondence systems to have their questions or concerns quickly addressed. The outreach program helped OSHA promote health and safety to hard-to-reach workers and to respond to concerns about worker health voiced by the public.

4.7   Injury and Illness Reporting

BP and government agencies engaged in unprecedented levels of activity to document injuries and illnesses during the Gulf oil spill response. OSHA required BP to keep a comprehensive incident-wide log that recorded cases, including those that did not require first aid, those that did require first aid, and the traditional OSHA recordable cases (those that required more than first aid). BP reported OSHA recordable and non-recordable illnesses and injuries during daily conference calls beginning the first week of May. BP provided OSHA and NIOSH recordable and non-recordable injury and illness data, and OSHA posted this data on its website.

4.8   OSHA's Support of Department of Labor Objectives

The Department of Labor made it a priority to ensure that BP hired locally available workers. For example, DOL's Employment and Training Administration (ETA) worked with the One-Stop Career Centers in the affected area to help facilitate the hiring and training of displaced workers. ETA published guidance and regularly communicated with state and local agencies. OSHA added information on the One-Stop Career Centers to its communication materials and highlighted them during community meetings. OSHA ensured that these workers, many of whom had no prior experience or training for cleaning up oil spills, received the protective equipment and training they needed to safely perform response and cleanup operations.

4.9   Summary of Activities

The workers on the front lines of the Deepwater Horizon response faced significant hazards on the job, such as electrical hazards, motor vehicle hazards, extreme heat, fatigue, sharp objects, material handling, confined spaces, potential chemical exposures, loud noises, drowning, struck-by, slips, falls, and insect bites. OSHA's effort included a comprehensive assessment of hazards and persistent oversight of BP to ensure that workers had the training and protection they needed. OSHA's activities were guided by its strategic objectives for the response: to continually monitor BP's efforts to ensure protection of all workers from all hazards, to reach out to communities to ensure that workers knew their rights, and to ensure that all workers were adequately trained for their jobs in a manner and language they understood. Through this oversight and monitoring, OSHA held BP accountable for worker health and safety, and OSHA and BP personnel were able to prevent, rapidly identify, and correct health and safety hazards in the numerous cleanup and response activities conducted over a wide geographic area.

Appendix A. Background on the Incident, the National Response System, and OSHA's Roles/Authority/Jurisdiction

A.1   The Deepwater Horizon Incident

On the night of April 20, 2010, the Deepwater Horizon oil rig, located 45 miles offshore southeast of Venice, LA, exploded and caught fire, resulting in the deaths of 11 workers. On the morning of April 22, 2010, the rig sank with approximately 700,000 gallons of diesel fuel onboard. The initial Coast Guard search-and-rescue response quickly evolved into a coordinated, interagency oil spill response when the National Response Team (NRT), which includes the Department of Labor (DOL) and the Occupational Safety and Health Administration (OSHA), was activated on April 22, 2010. Per the National Contingency Plan (NCP), the Coast Guard assumed the roles, duties, and responsibilities of the Federal On-Scene Coordinator (FOSC). Within days of the rig sinking, officials discovered that the Macondo wellhead, which was located 5,000 feet below the ocean surface, was discharging crude oil into the Gulf of Mexico.

On Thursday, April 29, the Secretary of Homeland Security announced that the incident would be designated a Spill of National Significance (SONS), which led to the appointment of a National Incident Commander (Admiral Thad Allen) to coordinate strategic planning and response issues at the national level. The Deepwater Horizon oil spill, the first oil spill incident in U.S. history to be declared a SONS, was unprecedented in both its scope and duration. The continuous discharge of oil from the well from April 22 until July 15, 2010, did not produce a single large uniform spill, but rather thousands of smaller disconnected spills that repeatedly threatened hundreds of miles of coastline of five Gulf Coast States—Louisiana, Mississippi, Alabama, Florida, and Texas. Working closely with interagency partners, including DOL and OSHA, at the local, regional, and national levels, the Coast Guard directed monumental response and cleanup efforts, including more than 47,000 workers and over 6,400 vessels, to remove and mitigate damages from the estimated 4.9 million barrels of oil discharged into the Gulf.

A.2   Overview of the National Response System

SUMMARY: The **National Contingency Plan** is a regulation establishing an organizational structure and procedures for responding to oil spills in U.S. waters. The organizational structure and set of procedures is known as the **National Response System.**

A.2.1 The National Contingency Plan

The National Oil and Hazardous Substances Pollution Contingency Plan, commonly called the National Contingency Plan (NCP) describes how the federal government responds to discharges of oil and the release of chemicals into the navigable waters or environment of the United States. The NCP, contained in regulations at 40 CFR 300, provides the organizational structure and procedures for preparing for and responding to oil spills.

A.2.2 The National Response System

The NCP established the National Response System (NRS). The NRS provides for a coordinated response by all levels of government to a real or potential oil or hazardous substances incident. It functions through a network of government agencies and private sector organizations. This federal coordination ensures that all stakeholders with jurisdiction over an incident have a place at the table and work together effectively. Under the NRS, the U.S. Environmental Protection Agency (EPA) is the lead agency for inland areas, and the U.S. Coast Guard is the lead agency for coastal areas and major navigable waterways.

Key components of the NRS include the **NRT,** the **FOSC, Regional Response Teams,** and the **responsible party,** as described below.

The **NRT** is made up of 16 federal departments and agencies, including DOL/OSHA. The NRT is responsible for coordinating nationwide interagency planning, policy, and response for oil and hazardous materials releases in support of the FOSC.

> ➤ *The Coast Guard activated the NRT, including DOL/OSHA, on April 22, 2010.*

National Response Team Members

U.S. Environmental Protection Agency (National Response Team Chair)

U.S. Coast Guard (National Response Team Vice Chair)

U.S. Department of Agriculture

U.S. Department of Labor/OSHA

U.S. Department of Commerce/National Oceanic and Atmospheric Administration

U.S. Department of State

U.S. Department of Defense

U.S. Department of Homeland Security

U.S. Department of Energy

U.S. Federal Emergency Management Agency

U.S. Department of Health and Human Services

U.S. General Services Administration

U.S. Department of the Interior

U.S. Nuclear Regulatory Commission

U.S. Department of Justice

U.S. Department of Transportation

Other Federal agencies with appropriate jurisdiction or expertise, along with private sector responders, may also support response efforts.

The **FOSC** is the lead federal official with final decision-making authority in the spill response. The Coast Guard provides an On-Scene Coordinator for oil spills in coastal waters, while EPA provides the On-Scene Coordinator for spills on land.

> ➤ *The Coast Guard designated Rear Admiral Mary Landry, Commander of the Eighth Coast Guard District, as the FOSC for the Deepwater Horizon oil spill on April 23, 2010.*

Regional Response Teams consist of regional representatives of each agency in the National Response team, state governments, and local governments. There are 13 Regional Response Teams, one for each of the 10 federal regions plus one each for Alaska, the Caribbean, and Oceana. The Regional Response Team does not deploy as a team to incident sites. Instead, its members reach back to their organizations for needed resources, and individual members may deploy to the site as resources from their agencies. The Regional Response Team also oversees and reviews plans within a region.

> ➤ *Two Regional Response Teams were active in the BP Deepwater Horizon oil spill response, corresponding to the two regions involved:*
>
> o *Region 4: Mississippi, Alabama, Florida, Georgia, Tennessee, North Carolina, South Carolina, and Kentucky*
>
> o *Region 6: Arkansas, Louisiana, New Mexico, Oklahoma, and Texas*

The **responsible party** is in charge of preparing for, responding to, and paying for cleanup and damages from its pollution incidents. The responsible party must follow procedures in its facility or vessel response plan, which provides for resources to respond to a "worst case" discharge.

> ➤ *BP was designated as the "responsible party" for the Deepwater Horizon incident.*

The National Contingency Plan vs. the Stafford Act

The role of the federal government, differs under the National Contingency Plan and the Robert T. Stafford Disaster Relief and Emergency Assistance Act (the "Stafford Act"). When a governor determines that state and local resources are insufficient to handle an emergency response (for example, during Hurricane Katrina), he or she may ask the president to contribute federal aid under the Stafford Act by declaring an emergency or major disaster. The response is run by the state, supplemented with federal resources and financing. In contrast, under the National Contingency Plan, the federal government directs the response to oil spills through the FOSC and National Incident Command, and the state participates through the UC structure. The responsible party, rather than the taxpayer, pays for the response under the NCP.

A.3   Overview of the Incident/Unified Command System

SUMMARY: The NRT encourages the use of an **Incident Command System (ICS)** to manage oil spill response operations. The ICS establishes an on-scene organization within which different agencies operate. The ICS organization includes **incident command posts** and **unified commands** at the local level. For large spills like the BP Deepwater Horizon spill involving multiple jurisdictions, a **Unified Area Command** brings together the various agencies, the responsible party, and non-government responders. The Unified Area Command is responsible for overall management of the incident. In addition, the Commandant of the Coast Guard can designate a **National Incident Commander** and establish a **National Incident Command** if a SONS is declared in the coastal zone.

A.3.1   The Incident Command System

The federal response to the BP Deepwater Horizon oil spill used an Incident Command System (ICS). An ICS establishes an integrated organizational structure appropriate for the complexity and demands of an incident, without being hindered by jurisdictional boundaries. An ICS allows for inclusion of federal, state, local, and responsible party representatives. An ICS is organized around five major management activities: command, operations, planning, logistics, and finance/administration.

The U.S. Forest Service first developed the ICS in the 1970s, in the aftermath of devastating, fast-moving wildfires in California, where communication and management problems hindered the response. After the Exxon Valdez oil spill in 1989, the system was adapted to oil spill response operations. The Coast Guard and EPA use ICS to achieve the coordination needed to carry out an efficient, effective oil spill response.

A.3.2   Local Incident Command Posts/Unified Commands

Under an ICS, local incident command posts are established for front-line responders. Incident command posts are usually located at or in the immediate vicinity of the incident site and are the focus for the direct, on-scene tactical operations. When a response requires that multiple agencies work together, the leadership of an ICS organization may be expanded into a unified command (Figure 1). Agencies work together through their designated members of the unified command to establish a common set of objectives and strategies and a single Incident Action Plan.

> ➤ *The Coast Guard, federal and state agencies, and BP set up local ICPs/unified commands in Houma, LA; Mobile, AL; St. Petersburg, FL; and Houston, TX (see Figure 1).*

A.3.3   Unified Area Command

A Unified Area Command is an organization set up to oversee the management of large incidents that cross jurisdictional boundaries and involve multiple agencies. It supervises the work of the Regional Response Teams and the local incident command posts/unified commands.

> *On April 23, when oil was first found to be leaking from the well riser and drill pipe, the Coast Guard established the Unified Area Command in Robert, LA. The Unified Area Command included senior representatives from the Coast Guard, the responsible party (BP), impacted states, and federal agencies involved in the oil spill response, including DOL/OSHA.*

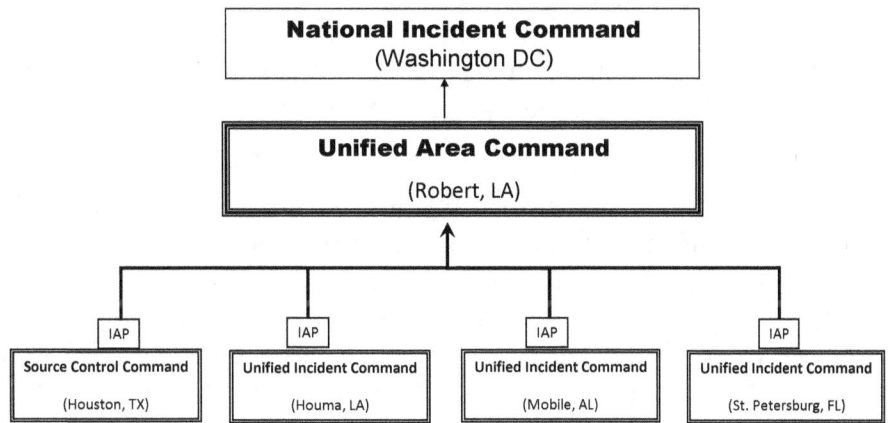

Figure 1. Deepwater Horizon Unified Command System

A.3.4 National Incident Commander

If an oil spill is classified as a SONS, the Coast Guard designates a National Incident Commander to take on the role of the On-Scene Coordinator in communicating with affected parties and the public, and coordinating federal, state, local, and international resources at the national level. The National Contingency Plan defines a SONS as "a spill which due to its severity, size, location, actual or potential impact on the public health and welfare or the environment, or the necessary response effort, is so complex that it requires extraordinary coordination of federal, state, local, and responsible party resources to contain and cleanup the discharge."

> *On April 29, 2010, the Coast Guard designated the disaster a Spill of National Significance, and named Admiral Thad Allen the National Incident Commander. This was the first spill ever designated a Spill of National Significance.*

A.3.5 National Incident Command

To support the National Incident Commander and achieve strategic unity of effort for the Deepwater Horizon oil spill response, on May 7 through September 30, 2010, the Coast Guard established a National Incident Command (NIC) with more than 150 Coast Guard and interagency staff located at Coast Guard Headquarters in Washington, DC (Figure 1). The NIC included an Interagency Solutions Group, with all of the NRT agencies, including DOL/OSHA, represented by senior staff. The NIC Interagency Solutions Group staff facilitated close communications, coordination, and collaboration, as well as the resolution of interagency response issues, including those related to protecting the safety and health of response and cleanup workers.

A.4 OSHA's Roles/Authorities/Jurisdiction

A.4.1 Occupational Safety and Health Act

On December 29, 1970, the Occupational Safety and Health Act of 1970 (OSH Act) was promulgated to assure safe and healthful working conditions for working men and women. The OSH Act created the Occupational Safety and Health Administration, whose mission includes assuring the safety and health of America's workers by setting and enforcing standards; providing training, outreach, and education; establishing partnerships; and encouraging continual process improvement in workplace safety and health.

Under the OSH Act, employers are responsible for providing a safe and healthful workplace for their employees. The OSH Act covers private sector employers and their employees in the 50 states and certain territories and jurisdictions under federal authority. Although OSHA provisions cover the private sector only, 22 states and jurisdictions have their own OSHA-approved occupational safety and health programs, which cover private sector employees and state and local government workers, and 5 which cover public employees only. (The Gulf Coast States affected by the Deepwater Horizon oil spill—Louisiana, Mississippi, Alabama, Florida, and Texas—do not have OSHA-approved State Plans and therefore fall under federal OSHA standards and requirements.) The OSH Act also requires federal agencies to comply with standards consistent with those for private sector employers.

A.4.1.1 OSHA Standards

In general, OSHA standards require that employers:

- Maintain conditions or adopt practices reasonably necessary and appropriate to protect workers.

- Be familiar with and comply with standards applicable to their establishments.

- Ensure that employees have and use personal protective equipment when required to protect their safety and health.

OSHA issues standards for a wide variety of workplace hazards, including toxic substances, harmful physical agents, electrical hazards, fall hazards, fire and explosion hazards, dangerous atmospheres, confined spaces, hazardous waste, machine hazards, and infectious diseases. In addition, where there are no specific OSHA standards, employers must comply with the OSH Act's "general duty clause." The general duty clause, section 5(a)(1) of the OSH Act, requires that each employer "furnish…a place of employment which [is] free from recognized hazards that are causing or are likely to cause death or serious physical harm to his employees."

Hazardous Waste Operations and Emergency Response

Because of the seriousness of the safety and health hazards related to hazardous waste operations and emergency response to hazardous substances, OSHA issued its Hazardous Waste Operations and Emergency Response (HAZWOPER) standard, Title 29 Code of

Federal Regulations (CFR) Parts 1910.120, to protect employees in this environment and to help them handle hazardous substances safely and effectively. In addition to hazardous waste site cleanup operations, the HAZWOPER standard covers employers and employees conducting emergency response and cleanup operations for hazardous substance releases, which includes oil spills.

Under the HAZWOPER standard, employers must develop and implement comprehensive safety and health programs with the following components:

- Organizational structure
- Comprehensive workplan
- Site-specific health and safety plan
- Emergency response plan
- Safety and health training program
- Medical surveillance program
- Standard operating procedures
- Site characterization and analysis
- Exposure monitoring
- Engineering controls
- Safe work practices
- Personal protective equipment (PPE) if needed
- Handling/labeling of drums and containers
- Decontamination procedures

Personal Protective Equipment

OSHA requires that employers protect their employees from workplace hazards that can cause injury. Controlling a hazard at its source is the best way to protect employees. When engineering, work practice, and administrative controls are not feasible or do not provide sufficient protection, employers must provide PPE to their employees and ensure its proper use and care. PPE is equipment worn to minimize exposure to a variety of hazards. Examples include gloves, foot and eye protection, protective hearing devices (e.g., earplugs, muffs), hard hats, respirators, and protective clothing/suits. Specific requirements for PPE are explained in many different OSHA standards published in 29 CFR, as shown below.

OSHA Requirements for PPE

- 29 CFR 1910.120 (HAZWOPER regulations have PPE requirements)

- 29 CFR 1910.132 (general requirements)

- 29 CFR 1910.133 (eye and face protection)

- 29 CFR 1910.134 (respiratory protection)

- 29 CFR 1910.135 (head protection)

- 29 CFR 1910.136 (foot protection)

- 29 CFR 1910.137 (electrical protective equipment)

- 29 CFR 1910.138 (hand protection)

- 29 CFR 1926 (construction industry regulations have PPE requirements)

- 29 CFR 1915 (maritime industry regulations have PPE requirements)

Respiratory Protection

When toxic substances are present in the workplace and engineering and work practice controls are inadequate to reduce or eliminate them, workers may need to wear respirators to reduce exposures. Respirators have limitations and are not a substitute for effective engineering and work practice controls. Respirator use may increase heat stress and strain a worker's heart and lungs. When respirators are required to protect workers' health, specific procedures are necessary to ensure the equipment's effectiveness. OSHA's respiratory protection standard (29 CFR 1910.134) requires employers to establish and maintain an effective respiratory protection program when employees must wear respirators to protect against workplace hazards. The standard contains requirements for program administration; worksite-specific procedures; respirator selection; employee training; fit testing; medical evaluation; and respirator use, cleaning, maintenance, and repair. Employers must fully train employees in all aspects of the respiratory protection program.

A.4.1.2   Jurisdictional Issues

Section 4(a) of the OSH Act limits the application of the Act to work performed in a U.S. state or territory or in facilities covered under the Outer Continental Shelf (OCS) Lands Act. A workplace in a state or territory can be on land, inland waters, or on waters within the state territorial limit, which is 3 miles for most states (except Texas and the Gulf coast of Florida, where the state territorial limit is 9 miles). The OCS Lands Act applies only to structures or facilities fixed to the ocean floor, not to vessels travelling over the OCS. Per section 4(b)(1) of the OSH Act, OSHA is preempted from regulating any working condition (e.g., occupational risk/hazard) addressed by requirements of another federal agency. Although the OCS Lands Act applies to certain working conditions on OCS Lands, it does not apply to working conditions with respect to which the Coast Guard or other federal agencies, including the Bureau of Ocean Energy Management, Regulation and Enforcement (formerly called the Minerals Management Service), exercise statutory authority to prescribe or enforce standards affecting occupational safety and health. Hence, for oil rigs located on the OCS, OSHA authority and regulations apply only for safety and health hazards not covered by other agency regulations.

Memorandum of Understanding Between the Coast Guard and OSHA Concerning Occupational Safety and Health on the Outer Continental Shelf

On December 19, 1979, the Coast Guard and OSHA signed a Memorandum of Understanding (MOU) to establish procedures to increase consultation and coordination between the agencies with respect to matters affecting the occupational safety and health of personnel working on the OCS of the United States. The MOU specifies that OSHA will cooperate with the Coast Guard to maximize the safety and health protection of employees, avoid duplication of effort, and avoid undue burdens on the maritime industry.

A.4.2 Worker Safety and Health in the National Contingency Plan

The National Response System, including the NRT and the National Contingency Plan (NCP), fully incorporates and addresses worker safety and health issues, including planning for, responding to, and recovery from oil and hazardous substances that fall under the NCP.

The Response Operations section of the NCP (40 CFR 300.135, paragraph 1) states that the FOSC is responsible for addressing worker health and safety concerns at a response scene, in accordance with part 300.150. In addition, 40 CFR 300.135(h) specifically states that the FOSC may call on OSHA for assistance on worker health and safety issues. Per 40 CFR 300.135(a), the FOSC is ultimately responsible for directing response efforts throughout the entire response area.

Section 40 CFR 300.150 of the NCP incorporates the OSHA HAZWOPER standard and addresses worker safety and health requirements, including those of the responsible party, as follows:

> (a) Response actions under the NCP will comply with the provisions for response action worker safety and health in 29 CFR 1910.120 (OSHA HAZWOPER regulations). The National Response System meets the requirements of 29 CFR 1910.120 concerning use of an incident command system.

> (b) In a response action taken by a responsible party, the responsible party must assure that an occupational safety and health program consistent with 29 CFR 1910.120 is made available for the protection of workers at the response site.

Under the NCP (40 CFR 300.170), federal departments/agencies, including DOL/OSHA, may be called upon by the FOSC during response planning and implementation (e.g., response operations) to provide assistance in their particular areas of expertise, as further described in 40 CFR 300.175, consistent with the agencies' capabilities and authorities. The NCP—40 CFR 300.175(b)(11)—specifically addresses OSHA's duties and responsibilities, which include providing technical assistance and support to the FOSC as well as fulfilling OSHA's normal duties, roles, and responsibilities under the OSH Act. **In no way does the NCP limit OSHA's existing statutory enforcement authority,** as shown by the following NCP citation from 40 CFR 300.175(b)(11)(ii):

> On request, OSHA will provide advice and consultation to EPA and other NRT/RRT agencies as well as to the OSC/RPM regarding hazards to persons engaged in response activities. OSHA may also take any other action necessary to assure that employees are properly protected at such response activities.

A.4.3 OSHA's Role in the Deepwater Horizon Oil Spill Response

As a member of the NRT, OSHA was activated on April 22, 2010, as part of the multi-agency, coordinated federal response to the Deepwater Horizon oil spill. As described in Section A.4.2 of this Appendix, OSHA was requested to provide technical assistance and support to the FOSC (the Coast Guard), working within the UC, to protect the safety and health of response and cleanup workers. OSHA's technical assistance role during a SONS is guided by comprehensive national policies contained in the NCP, OSHA Directives, and other legal authorities.

Per the Coast Guard's request, OSHA's technical assistance and support role covered all Deepwater Horizon response and cleanup workers throughout the incident's wide geographical area. This did not limit or constrain OSHA in executing its regulatory and enforcement authorities under the OSH Act, as explained in Section A.4.2. While providing technical assistance and support to the FOSC for worker safety and health issues and concerns, OSHA provided aggressive oversight of the responsible party (BP) throughout the incident to ensure that BP was providing a safe and healthful workplace for their employees—the response and cleanup workers they hired—as required by the OSH Act.

A.4.3.1   Technical Assistance/Support Roles and Enforcement

Under the OSH Act, OSHA's primary duty is to ensure that employers are taking necessary actions to protect employees from work-related hazards on the job. Enforcement of standards is an important means provided by the OSH Act to achieve this end. However, as described below, this enforcement role may not always be the most effective means of ensuring that employers protect workers during an incident of national significance, when OSHA is requested to provide technical assistance and support to the FOSC and the UC.

During the Deepwater Horizon response, workers benefited from OSHA's technical assistance role within the UC. OSHA actively monitored BP's development of site safety and health plans, provision of training, and voluntary abatement of hazards, including where no OSHA standard existed (e.g., heat stress). This vigorous intervention was possible, in part, because in its technical assistance role, OSHA had unlimited access to the workers and employers involved in the cleanup activities. By working within the UC in a technical assistance role, hazards can be quickly abated. OSHA's enforcement role can lead to litigation and potentially delay abatement of hazards.

Furthermore, when operating in the technical assistance role, OSHA can encourage employers to protect workers to a higher degree than the legally enforceable standards. For example, In the Deepwater Horizon response, OSHA worked with the UC to use the most protective occupational exposure limits to monitor and protect workers from chemical exposures rather than solely enforcing the OSHA Permissible Exposure Limits.

A.4.3.2 Memorandum of Understanding Between OSHA and the Federal On-Scene Coordinator Concerning Occupational Safety and Health Issues

On June 6, 2010, the Assistant Secretary of Labor for OSHA and the FOSC (Coast Guard) developed and signed an MOU to establish procedures for consultation and coordination between the FOSC and OSHA on matters affecting the safety and health of workers involved in the Deepwater Horizon oil spill.

The MOU reinforces the authorities, duties, and responsibilities of OSHA under the NCP and the OSH Act. It also provides guidelines for information-sharing between the agencies, including procedures for referrals and OSHA enforcement actions, if needed.

See Appendix C for a copy of the MOU.

Appendix B. Deepwater Horizon Oil Spill Response—OSHA Chronology Through June 25

<u>**Week of April 19–25**</u>

April 20—Fire and explosion on Deepwater Horizon rig resulting in 11 worker deaths. The site of the release is approximately 50 miles off shore of Louisiana, well outside OSHA's jurisdiction. OSHA, however, initiates monitoring of the situation, anticipating that the oil will likely approach the shoreline and involve cleanup workers on or just off shore who will fall under OSHA's jurisdiction

April 22—OSHA's National Office receives a notice activating the National Response Team (NRT). The Secretary of Labor's Office is briefed about the incident by OSHA in preparation of a White House briefing.

April 23—White House Situation Room briefing attended by OSHA staff.

April 24—NRT begins daily conference calls, initially led by DHS Secretary Napolitano, to provide situational updates to the NRT member agencies. OSHA participates in these calls throughout the oil spill response.

<u>**Week of April 26–May 2**</u>

OSHA's NRT Regional Response Teams in Regions 4 (Atlanta) and 6 (Dallas) activated and representatives are deployed to the Unified Area Command Center in Robert, LA, and the Unified Incident Command Centers in Houma, LA, and Mobile, AL. Discussions begin on level of protective training required for oil spill cleanup workers.

OSHA participates in daily conference calls with BP officials in Unified Incident Command Centers in Houma, LA, and Mobile, AL, and includes OSHA's National and Regional Emergency Management personnel.

April 28—OSHA staff first sent to Venice, LA, to monitor worker protections at staging operation (Venice is the first of the staging areas that OSHA monitored).

April 30—OSHA personnel staff the begin liaison with Unified Area Command in Robert, LA. OSHA personnel first sent to Pascagoula and Biloxi, MS, staging areas and shoreline of Alabama to monitor worker protection. OSHA staff continually return to review working conditions and to monitor training programs.

April 30—OSHA begins review of BP's proposed training program for those involved in the cleanup of contaminated materials.

May 1—OSHA provides staff for Mobile Unified Command to monitor safety and health protection for workers.

May 1—OSHA Assistant Secretary David Michaels invites representatives of NIOSH and the National Institute of Environmental Health Sciences (NIEHS) to collaborate with OSHA on cleanup worker protection efforts.

May 2—Initial Safety and Health Plan reviewed and approved.

May 2—OSHA staff sent to Pensacola, FL, to assess situation.

Week of May 3–May 9

May 3—Dr. Michaels and OSHA staff, together with NIOSH, NIEHS, and EPA, travel to Louisiana to meet with Coast Guard Rear Admiral Landry and representatives of BP to discuss preparations for protecting workers as the oil moved towards the shore. These meetings are the beginning of a close collaboration between these four public health agencies that continue throughout the cleanup effort. At the meetings, OSHA discusses again with BP that cleanup workers will need to be trained according to OSHA requirements, that local people will have to be hired for work in the cleanup efforts, and that training will have to be done in the language the workers understand.

OSHA launches public web site: "Keeping Workers Safe During Oil Spill Response and Cleanup Operations."

From May 3 onward, OSHA participates in daily conference calls with BP officials in Unified Incident Command Centers in Houma, LA, and Mobile, AL (and includes OSHA's National and Regional Emergency Management personnel).

May 4—OSHA staff first sent to Panama City staging area to monitor safety and health protections for workers. OSHA staff continually return to review working conditions.

May 5—OSHA approves BP's 4-hour training program with recommendations for improvement.

May 5—BP begins its 4-hour (Module 3) training program. All workers hired by BP and its contractors to clean up spill contaminated shoreline and vessel operations are required to complete this training prior to starting work. Module 3 includes safety and health management, hazards and controls, including PPE requirements. (Module 1 training is the BP Health and Safety Basic Orientation [45 minutes] and Module 2 is Contractor Expectations [1.5 hours]. Both Module 1 and Module 2 are for workers not involved in cleaning up oil contaminated debris). Emphasis is placed on ensuring that workers are trained in a language and vocabulary they understand. OSHA, along with NIEHS, continues to monitor this program providing daily oversight on the BP training. (Note that all work crews on shore and on vessels are supervised by individuals with 40-hour HAZWOPER training.)

May 6—OSHA's Health Response Team (from Salt Lake City) arrives in Louisiana to provide industrial hygiene support to OSHA response onsite personnel.

May 7—OSHA deploys senior staff to National Incident Command Interagency Solutions Group at the U.S. Coast Guard headquarters. OSHA has continued agency representation at this critical post throughout the crisis.

May 8—OSHA personnel in Houma review BP's Offshore Sampling Plan.

HEAT: By the first week in May, OSHA is requiring BP to institute a heat stress mitigation plan. From this point to the end of OSHA's involvement in the oil spill response, heat stress remained one of OSHA's primary health concerns. OSHA raised these concerns with BP and required that BP implement protective measures including tents, water, rest breaks, and sunburn protection.

By the end of this week, OSHA had 20 staff in the field assigned solely to the Gulf response. During the next three months, OSHA would have between 20 and 40 staff assigned every day. OSHA was on the boats and in the field ensuring that BP and its contractors were protecting workers from health and safety hazards.

Week of May 10–May 16

OSHA personnel in Houma review BP's direct reading sampling results for offshore vessels and continue this throughout the spill.

May 11—OSHA and NIEHS complete a joint pocket booklet that details health and safety concerns and protections for oil spill response workers. The booklet contains information on heat injury prevention, health risks of weathered oil, PPE requirements and general health and safety topics (e.g., fatigue). The booklet is sent for translation into Spanish and Vietnamese. 15,000 pocket-sized booklets are printed and distributed in all three languages.

May 13—Dr. Michaels meets with Dr. David C. Nagle, Executive Vice President of BP America, Inc., to discuss BP's worker safety and health efforts. Deepwater Horizon/Mississippi Canyon 252 Oil Spill Fact Sheet finalized.

May 13—BP reports on daily call 952 personnel trained in Module 3.

May 14—OSHA publishes the OSHA Deepwater Horizon/Mississippi Canyon 252 Oil Spill Fact Sheet. The factsheet addresses hazards during shoreline and vessel operations, training, PPE requirements and employer responsibilities. The factsheet is subsequently translated into Spanish and Vietnamese for distribution. Copies are distributed at all staging areas.

May 14—BP reports on daily call 1370 personnel trained in Module 3.

Week of May 17–23

OSHA participates in weekly calls to stakeholders on health and safety concerns in the Gulf. The call is with 200 NGO's coordinated by CEQ.

May 20—The Incident Command Post in Houma reports shoreline impact at Marsh Island. Tar balls also sighted on Long Beach, MS.

May 21—Dr. Michaels telephones Mr. David Nagle to make him aware of numerous deficiencies in BP's oil spill response operations related to worker safety and health. Dr. Michaels indicates his resolve to take all necessary actions to ensure that BP meets its obligation to protect workers. OSHA is especially concerned that BP is not correcting identified problems.

May 21—BP reports in a daily call that 10,000 personnel have been trained in Module 3.

Week of May 24–30

OSHA begins weekly call solely focused on worker health and safety issues with stakeholders.

May 24—OSHA staff begin taking exposure samples off the coast of Louisiana, initiating the agency's own independent worker exposure sampling plan.

May 24—Dr. Michaels speaks with Coast Guard leadership to make them aware of the level of concern OSHA has regarding BP's commitment to protecting its workers.

May 25—Dr. Michaels sends a memorandum to Admiral Thad Allen, the Coast Guard's National Incident Commander, re-emphasizing OSHA's concerns with BP's systems in place for worker protection.

May 26—OSHA launches investigation into the illnesses of seven fishermen sent to the hospital.

May 27—In response to the reports of the seven fishermen who were sent to the hospital, OSHA and NIOSH use the daily conference call to inform BP of the procedures to request a Health Hazard Evaluation (HHE) to have NIOSH fully investigate the cause of these illnesses. Later that day, BP requests that NIOSH conduct an HHE into all significant worker safety incidents during the oil spill cleanup to date. OSHA staff brief NIOSH on the situation. NIOSH arrives on June 2 to begin the investigation of the incident involving the seven fisherman and other incidents.

May 28—Unified sampling strategy posted on OSHA's public website.

Week of May 31–June 6

OSHA begins weekly set call with state health officials (prior to this, calls are held at various times).

May 29—Deputy Secretary Harris holds a phone conversation with ADM Allen regarding worker safety/health issues. Both agree that an MOU/MOA between OSHA and the Coast Guard is warranted.

May 31—OSHA's Deputy Assistant Secretary, Jordan Barab, goes to Louisiana to review OSHA's response efforts, speak with oil spill cleanup workers, and assist in the coordination with Coast Guard. Mr. Barab is part of a delegation that includes NIOSH Director John Howard, U.S. Surgeon General Regina Benjamin, Health and Human Services Assistant Secretary for Preparedness and Response, Nicole Lurie, NIEHS Worker Education and Training Program Director Joseph Hughes, and OSHA staff. OSHA is on the front lines of ensuring that BP and its contractors protect workers from hazards. Barab inspects beach cleanup operations in Port Fourchon and Vessel of Opportunity operations in Venice. He interviews workers in both locations about health and safety training and working conditions.

June 2—OSHA instructs BP to increase the level of training provided to workers involved with the marine cleanup who are involved in oil skimming operations as well as operations that require contact with oil-soaked boom. These workers are having greater contact with the weathered oil. OSHA requests that NIEHS participate in curriculum development. OSHA and NIEHS provide oversight and direction to BP on the curriculum. NIEHS will conduct the training.

June 7—OSHA posts initial data from independent worker exposure monitoring on this website. As new data are available, they are added to the site. The data are accompanied by a narrative and sampling protocol.http://www.osha.gov/oilspills/oil_directreading_bysite.html

June 9—OSHA personnel sent to staff Robert, LA, Unified Area Command.

June 9—Secretary of Labor Hilda L. Solis and Dr. Michaels travel to Louisiana to inspect efforts to ensure the health, safety, and well-being of workers affected by the BP oil spill. They meet with beach cleanup workers in Port Fourchon and discuss worker safety with OSHA staff in Houma, LA. The Secretary and OSHA staff hold meetings with community organizations. This outreach, begun in May, continues throughout the cleanup.

June 25—NIOSH and OSHA issue recommendations that workers in the close vicinity of crude oil burns have access to respirators and receive appropriate training and medical evaluation in case wind shifts or other unexpected problems bring workers into the smoke plume. No cases of oil burn workers being caught in the smoke plume were ever reported. Throughout the response, OSHA identified no exposures that exceeded any of the most recent, lowest, and most protective exposure limits set by organizations such as NIOSH, ACGIH, and AIHA for hazardous chemicals.

Appendix C. Memorandum of Understanding (MOU) Between OSHA and the Federal On-Scene Coordinator (FOSC) Concerning Occupational Safety and Health Issues

MEMORANDUM OF UNDERSTANDING

BETWEEN THE

OCCUPATIONAL SAFETY AND HEALTH ADMINISTRATION,

DEPARTMENT OF LABOR

AND THE

FEDERAL ON SCENE COORDINATOR,

DEPARTMENT OF HOMELAND SECURITY

CONCERNING OCCUPATIONAL SAFETY AND HEALTH ISSUES RELATED TO THE DEEPWATER HORIZON OIL SPILL RESPONSE

I. PURPOSE AND BACKGROUND – The purpose of this Memorandum of Understanding is to establish procedures for consultation and coordination between the Federal On Scene Coordinator (FOSC) and Occupational Safety and Health Administration (OSHA) with respect to matters affecting the occupational safety and health of workers involved in the response to the Deepwater Horizon oil spill (the "oil spill"). OSHA and the FOSC recognize the importance of close cooperation and coordination among all agencies with responsibilities for response activities.

OSHA and U.S. Coast Guard (USCG) have a long history of working cooperatively to protect workers. As set forth in two longstanding MOUs, the agencies cooperate in determining coverage, scheduling inspections, and investigating accidents, among other issues.

This cooperation between OSHA and USCG has continued since the beginning of this oil spill. For example, OSHA, working through the Unified Area Command, has been disseminating information about necessary safety and health precautions to BP. BP is the Responsible Party under the National Contingency Plan (40 C.F.R. Part 300) (the "NCP") and the Oil Pollution Act of 1990 and is liable for all response costs and damages from the oil spill (*See e.g.* 33 U.S.C. 2702). OSHA has also provided this information to BP's contractors that employ the workers involved in oil spill response. OSHA has also been assuring that workers receive appropriate training and that they use proper personal protective equipment, and is taking other actions to assure overall worker heath and safety.

II. AUTHORITY – On April 22, 2010, the National Response Team was activated pursuant to the NCP and a Federal On Scene Coordinator was appointed. On or about April 29 the oil spill was declared a Spill of National Significance pursuant to the NCP and Admiral Thad Allen was appointed as the National Incident Commander. Under the NCP, all response actions must comply with OSHA's Hazardous Waste and Emergency Response Standard, 29 C.F.R. 1910.120, as well as other relevant OSHA requirements. (*See* NCP, 40 C.F.R. 300.150 – Worker Health and Safety).

The responsibilities of the Federal On Scene Coordinator include, without limitation, the authority to direct all response efforts and coordinate all other efforts at the scene of a discharge or release. (*See e.g.,* 40 C.F.R. 300.120; 300.135). The National Incident Commander may assume the role of the Federal On Scene Coordinator in communicating with affected parties and the public, and coordinating federal, state, local and international resources at the national level. (*See* 40 C.F.R. 300.323)

The duties and responsibilities of Federal agencies are generally set forth in the NCP at 40 C.F.R. 300.175. The Department of Labor, through OSHA and the states operating plans approved under section 18 of the OSH Act, 29 U.S.C. 667, has authority to conduct safety and health inspections to assure that employees are being protected and to determine if the site is in compliance with safety and health standards and regulations promulgated under the OSH Act and its general duty clause. (*See* 40 C.F.R. 300.175(b)(11)). In addition, OSHA may take any other action necessary to assure that employees are properly protected, and may provide advice and consultation to the FOSC and other agencies in the NRT. *Id.* The NCP does not limit OSHA's existing statutory enforcement authority. (*See* 40 C.F.R. 300.150(e)).

III. INFORMATION SHARING – The FOSC and OSHA will share relevant information with each other, while ensuring that the exchange of such information complies with applicable law.

A. Referrals – If either the FOSC or OSHA learns of potential hazards or other conditions of concern within the other agency's responsibility or authority, it shall notify the other agency promptly. This includes information it learns of directly, in its own response activities, as well as information received from other parties, including workers, local government officials, or anyone else.

B. Enforcement – OSHA will notify the FOSC when it intends to take any enforcement action against BP, BP's contractors, or any other employer engaged in response activities. This may include action in response to imminent dangers, other serious hazards, fatalities or catastrophes, serious injuries or illnesses, or other situations where OSHA determines enforcement is necessary to protect worker safety or health.

C. Press and Public Statements – The FOSC and OSHA will notify each other about planned press releases, press conferences, and other public statements related to the occupational safety and health of workers involved in oil spill response.

D. Other Information – The FOSC and OSHA will also share any other information relevant to the subject of this MOU.

E. The Assistant Secretary or his designee and the FOSC or his designee will be responsible for the communications described in this section.

IV. EFFECTIVE DATE

This Memorandum is effective upon signature by the parties. It may be amended at any time by mutual written agreement of the agencies and may be terminated by either agency upon thirty days written notice.

V. EFFECT OF AGREEMENT

This agreement is an internal Government agreement and is not intended to confer any right upon any private person.

This agreement does not itself authorize the expenditure or reimbursement of any funds. Nothing in this agreement obligates the parties to expend appropriations or enter into any contract or other obligations.

Nothing in this Memorandum shall be deemed to alter, amend, or affect in any way the statutory or regulatory authority of the Federal On Scene Coordinator, the National Incident Commander (or any delegation of authority to these officers), the U.S. Coast Guard or OSHA.

This agreement will be executed in full compliance with the Privacy Act of 1974

[signature on file]

_____   06/08/2010

DAVID MICHAELS   Date

Assistant Secretary for Occupational

  Safety and Health

U.S. Department of Labor

[signature on file]

_____   06/06/2010

JAMES WATSON, RADM, USCG   Date

Federal On Scene Coordinator

U.S. Department of Homeland Security

Appendix D. Acronyms

D.1 Agencies and Actors

DHS	U.S. Department of Homeland Security
ETA	Employment and Training Administration
EPA	U.S. Environmental Protection Agency
HHS	U.S. Department of Health and Human Services
NIEHS	National Institute of Environmental Health Sciences, National Institutes of Health, U.S. Department of Health and Human Services
NIOSH	National Institute for Occupational Safety and Health, Centers for Disease Control and Prevention, U.S. Department of Health and Human Services
NOAA	National Oceanic and Atmospheric Administration, U.S. Department of Commerce
OSHA	Occupational Safety and Health Administration, U.S. Department of Labor

D.2 Deepwater Horizon and Emergency Response Terms

FOSC	Federal On-Scene Coordinator
ICP	Incident Command Post
ICS	Incident Command System
JIC	Joint Information Center
MOU	Memorandum of Understanding
NCP	National Contingency Plan (40 CFR 300)
NEMP	National Emergency Management Plan
NRF	National Response Framework
NRS	National Response System
NRT	National Response Team
NIC	National Incident Command
SONS	Spill of National Significance
UAC	Unified Area Command

| UC | Unified Command |

D.3 Safety and Health Terms

OEL	Occupational Exposure Limit
PEL	Permissible Exposure Limit
PPE	Personal Protective Equipment

D.4 Laws and Regulations

| HAZWOPER | OSHA Hazardous Waste Operations and Emergency Response regulations, 29 CFR 1910.120 |
| OSH Act | Occupational Safety and Health Act |